D0006693

Jim Bowie

A Texas Legend

Jim Bowie

A Texas Legend

By Jean Flynn

FOERSTER ELEMENTARY LIBRARY
14200 Fonmeadow Lane
Houston, Texas 77035

Drawings by Buddy Mullan

Stories
For Young Americans
Series

EAKIN PRESS ★ AUSTIN, TEXAS

FIRST EDITION

Copyright © 1980
By Jean Flynn

Published in the United States of America
By Eakin Press
An Imprint of Sunbelt Media, Inc.
P.O. Drawer 90159 ★ Austin, TX 78709-0159

ALL RIGHTS RESERVED. No part of this book may be reproduced in any form without written permission from
the publisher, except for brief passages included in a re-
view appearing in a newspaper or magazine.

ISBN 0-89015-241-1

Stories For Young Americans Series

My first book

for my first love,

Robert Lopez Flynn

Table of Contents

I

The Wild Bowie Boy

"Yah-hoo! I got him!" a voice roared from the trees. Jim Bowie was chasing an alligator again. He threw the rope over the long nose and jerked it tight as it slipped about half-way toward the eyes. The angry alligator kicked and flopped. Water splashed all over Jim. He didn't care. He kept dragging his catch toward him.

Jim began wading into the river. He wanted to stay in front of the alligator as long as possible. He had once seen a man's leg broken by an alligator's tail. He must keep the alligator in water too deep for its legs to touch bottom. Jim checked the depth of the water by his own legs. He couldn't go too deep. He had to be able to straddle the alligator's back without any help.

For Jim, riding an alligator was better than riding a wild bronc. He loved all the jumping and thrashing around. He had ridden enough to know how to hang on the wildest ones. Jim didn't want to miss an exciting ride. He straddled the alligator's back carefully keeping his bare feet out of the way of the thrashing legs and tail.

Feeling Jim's weight on its back, the alligator once again began to thrash around. Jim's eyes were as shiny as his wet hair. Long before he got tired of riding, Jim saw that he was headed for the river bank. There was no way to turn the alligator back to the middle of the river.

Jim jumped off as soon as he was in wading water. Now he really had to be quick. The rope had to come off the nose. His mama would get him good if he had to explain how he lost a rope. Before the alligator realized what had happened, Jim had loosened the rope and jerked it free of the nose. He scrambled up the river bank with the mad alligator right behind.

Jim was a character of action. He was a daredevil of fate. He lived in wild and violent times. Stories about "that wild Bowie boy" grew as the boy himself grew older. There were legends that grew from his life. But James Bowie was more than a Texas folktale. He came from a background of pioneers. He inherited his forefathers' spirit of adventure and the courage to follow it.

Reese Bowie, his grandfather, came to America in 1705. The settlement in South Carolina was quite different from his Scotch Hilander background. In Scotland, the Bowies had lived in an old established country. In America they faced the fears and excitement of the unknown.

They had little food when they arrived. There were no shelters to keep them out of the weather. They had never cleared raw land for farming. They did not know for sure what crops would grow. They heard rumors of wild Indians. But it was the excitement and the desire to build a new life and a new country that brought them to the strange new land.

Reese Bowie did not move westward. He had come far enough to satisfy his longing for adventure. He died in South Carolina. But his son John had inherited his father's adventurous spirit. Before he was twenty years old, John became a captain in the 5th South Carolina Cavalry during the American Revolution.

John believed in America's right to freedom. He took his orders to fight seriously. John asked no man under his orders to risk his life unless John led the battle. He was leading a night march to surprise a British troop when he was severely wounded. He was shot in the first line of fire. The wounds in his shoulder and arm were severe.

John lived in a half-unconcious state for days. He argued and fought to get out of bed. He dreamed the British were wearing white uniforms instead of red. He was furious that the white figure by his bed could hold him down.

It was only when John was rational that he discovered the white figure wasn't British. He looked into the face of Elve Jones. Southern ladies were called upon during the revolution to be as strong-willed as the men. Elve was a nurse tending to the wounded soldiers in Savanah, Georgia.

John, having a strong mind and good judgement, married Elve. Elve also had a strong mind. She was well-educated for a girl of her times. She and John were matched in intellect and courage. They had the brave spirits needed by frontier citizens.

There were many dangers in moving to a new land. Elve and John carried only as many supplies as they could load on their wagon. They had enough seeds to plant one crop of corn and cotton and a small garden. The first crop they planted would have to give them food and seed for another year. Their tools for work were few. There would be no way to replace lost or broken things in the wilderness. They left every comfort of home behind. Life would be harsh.

The Indians, who had at first befriended the settlers, were on the warpath. They were unhappy that the white man was taking over their land. The land was raw, uncultivated brush and trees. Nothing kept John and Elve from moving westward.

Elve and John worked side-by-side. With each move from Georgia to Tennessee to Missouri to Kentucky to Louisiana, they started with new land. They cleared the land of trees and built a house. Each house was a little larger than the last. The Bowie family was growing.

They barely cleared the land, built a house and added another child to their family until John was ready to go west again. With each move, the Bowies made a profit on their homestead. Since they sold for more than they paid, the extra money was invested in the next farm. Their last move was to Louisiana.

Elva and John were growing older. They were contented with their homestead. They would let their four sons and two daughters carry on the westward movement.

James, or Jim as he was called, was born in Elliot Springs, Tennessee, in 1795. Jim was the third son born to Elve and John. All three boys inherited their parents' adventurous spirit. The two daughters and youngest son did not have the desire to move away. They left the taming of the wild to the three older brothers.

Jim was the most adventurous of the three boys. He was also the most restless. From childhood he spent most of his time exploring and trying new things. By the time he was a teenager, he was known for roping and riding alligators. He was a constant worry to his mother. He feared nothing but his mother's anger.

Jim knew that to avoid his mother's anger he had to learn his daily lessons. There were no schools in the wild, unsettled country. Elve set up a school of her own for the Bowie children. The schoolroom was the kitchen. Elve gave assignments daily. The children sat on benches around the long, rough table. Elve insisted they do their lessons before anything else.

Jim didn't mind so much in the wintertime. In warm weather when he wanted to be outside, he rushed through his work. He learned quickly that the sooner he finished, the sooner he could slip away from the house.

One warm day the children were having a French lesson. Jim was restless. He was in and out of the house as often as Elve would excuse him. He could hardly sit still. Elve was by the fireplace fixing stew for their dinner. Jim slid his hands in both pockets and dropped something from each hand on the floor.

Two old bullfrogs hopped toward Elve. She turned around just as one of the frightened frogs jumped toward her. Elve screamed and grabbed the straw broom by the door. She almost beat the frogs to death before she knocked them out the door.

The children looked at each other. No one laughed. As they lowered their eyes to the table, Jim started chuckling. Jim's brothers and sisters could not hold back the laughter as Elve swatted Jim with the broom. She didn't need to ask. She knew who had done it.

Elve's home education was helpful to Jim all of his life. She was a demanding teacher and taught her children all she had learned. Jim learned to speak French and Spanish as well as how to read and write English. His ability to speak different languages won him many friends. His letters of later years proved him to be a well-educated man. He was quick and eager to learn new things. He was glad that his mother had insisted on his education.

Although Elve was strict on the education of the children, John was not so strict on the farm work. He worked the boys hard, but he allowed them free time to roam and explore. Jim was friendly and loved sports. He became an expert with the lasso. Neighbors were often entertained with his roping and riding wild horses. Tales began to spread about his alligator rides. The "wild Bowie boy" was known by all in the surrounding communities.

Jim was a mixture of personalities. He enjoyed the times of celebration among the settlers. He seemed to be a wild and rowdy boy who liked attention. He could stand company for only so long. He loved people, but he liked quiet times as well. He went into the swamps for days at a time to hunt and fish. When he tired of his own company, he returned home.

On one of his swamp expeditions, Jim was walking quietly through the brush looking for game. As he reached a small clearing, he realized he was not alone. The Indian squinted his eyes in the sunlight. His hands gripped his spear. Dark brown eyes looked deep into the white boy's face. Jim stood tall. His hand rested lightly on the hunting knife he always carried. Both were sizing up the opponent.

Jim raised his hand and smiled. The Indian brave slowly raised his hand to signal friendship. Jim made friends with the young Indian. The two hunted and fished together many times. Neither could speak the other's language, but they communicated in spirit. Jim's fearlessness spread among the Indians.

Jim's childhood was full and happy. He worked hard and long. He played equally hard and enthusiastically. He watched the wild country gradually become settled. Some families had stayed. Some had moved on west. Some who could not endure the hardships returned to their homes. Life was difficult only for the weak.

Jim lived a life of activity. He loved excitement. He explored the unknown. He feared nothing. He searched for adventure until the final adventure of his life—the Battle of the Alamo.

II

A Legend Begins

The settled life of John and Elve Bowie was not for Jim. His parents were happy in their Louisiana home. They were not wealthy, but they were comfortable. One by one their children were marrying and leaving home. Their house was as large and fine as they would ever need. The farmland was cleared and planted. Food was plentiful. They did not need many clothes. They had enough adventure. They were no longer interested in developing untamed land.

Resin, Jim's favorite brother, married at the age of nineteen. Jim was disgusted. "Why," he asked himself, "would Resin want to tie himself to a farm here?"

Jim had planned on Resin being his partner in new discoveries. Resin's marriage seemed to Jim to be the end of Resin's adventures.

Resin was a talker. Jim was a rebel and a doer. He wanted to be on his own. He wanted to own land, lots of land. His eyes sparkled as he dreamed of the fortune he could make farther west. He wasn't satisfied with his brothers' and parents' lives. His restless spirit would not stay still.

At the age of eighteen Jim began to seek his fortune. He was by that time a full grown man. He was a big man. Reddish-blond streaked hair topped a 6 foot 1 inch frame. There was nothing soft looking about him. The sun had burned his skin everywhere he wasn't covered by clothing. His hands were long and rough from farm work. Dark grey-blue eyes, deep-set in his head, flashed with determination.

Around 1814, Jim moved from his parents home to Bayou Boeuf. He was poor but proud. Jim looked at the land he had chosen. It was covered with trees. Before farming could begin, Jim had to clear the land. He was not discouraged as he looked at the work to be done.

Jim lay on his crudely made bed of leaves covered by animal skins. He looked toward the sky. He glimpsed patches of light blue beyond the tall pine trees. He watched squirrels jumping from limb to limb. He saw birds flittering in and out of the thick trees. He dreamed and planned.

He would clear the trees from the land. As each tree was sawed down, it could be trimmed and sold for lumber. Jim would need a raft to carry the lumber to New Orleans. The first trees cut would be used to make the raft. He could trim the branches from the trees and roll them to the river bank.

He would waste nothing. The small limbs and branches trimmed from the trees would make a shelter for the winter. He would save all animal hides to use for clothing and bedding. He would hunt and fish only when he needed food. He planned each step of his new business.

Had Jim not been so strong and stubborn, he could not have survived. The trees had to be sawed with a common whip ripsaw. The saw was long and thin with a jagged cutting edge. A crude handle was attached to the broadest end for pushing and pulling the saw through the tree. It was a one man operation.

Jim first cut the trees nearest the river. Each tree was trimmed and then rolled to the river bank. When he had enough trees, he built a raft. With each tree he rolled, Jim told himself he needed a mule. He could do twice the work if he had help in moving the lumber.

When it was too dark to cut trees, Jim sat by the firelight and worked. He was skilled in using his knife. He cut every scrap of animal skin for moccasins or straps. He hung his meat up to dry with odd sizes of straps. His clothing was put together at the seams with small strips of skin.

Jim seldom took time to hunt or fish. When a squirrel jumped in a tree near him, he killed it. He used either his gun or knife. If the animal were near enough, Jim threw his knife. Occasionally he shot a duck flying over the tree tops. He could hit his target with either weapon. He took time to fish only when he grew tired of game.

In warm weather he sometimes bathed in the river. His sharp eyes were always on the lookout for alligators in the muddy water. But he had no time for the wild rides of his youth. He wasn't worried about being hurt. Jim always assumed he would come out on top of whatever he did. He just didn't have time to play around. His entertainment was his daydreams as he worked. The work, he knew, would pay off in riches. Then he could be wild again.

For many people, life in the wilderness was too lonely to endure. For Jim it was like food for a hungry man. He never tired of it. He made a game of fighting the ticks, mosquitoes, and chiggers. Every one that he killed became imaginary money in his pocket.

Jim was obsessed with his lumber business. Never once did he doubt that he would one day be a wealthy, powerful man. Men would seek his advice about investments. He would be known by his reputation as a man of action. He would bow down to no one.

Jim watched a tree fall. His back was stiff from bending. His arms ached from pushing the saw back and forth. Perspiration poured down his face. With callous hands, he wiped the water from his eyes.

The tree was the last one to add to the stack Jim was making on the raft. His excitement had grown as the raft became stacked with logs. He was ready for his first try at being a businessman.

Jim's first trip to New Orleans with lumber was a scarey one. He knew there was danger from alligators as well as Indians. He had to keep a sharp lookout for movement in the water and along the banks of the river. And he had heard that a man could be killed for a dollar in New Orleans.

New Orleans was a new world to Jim. In his wildest dreams, he had never pictured the excitement of the town. Everywhere he looked, structures were being built. He saw that the demand for lumber was great. Little bargaining was done when Jim sold his lumber. He simply sold to the highest price offered. He agreed to provide lumber in the future. He was now a real businessman.

Jim felt like a new man with money in his pocket. He was ready to explore the city. The old-timers watched the big stranger take long strides down the street. Jim looked the typical back woodsman. His clothes were dirty and torn. His hair was long and shaggy. His handsome face was covered with a matted, red beard. There was nothing about him to warn thieves to stay clear of him. They did not know that big man was as quick as a cat.

Two friendly looking, well-dressed men spoke to him. They began walking beside him. Jim's deep-set eyes missed nothing. He saw the look between the two men when he told them he was in the lumber business. He saw their smiles when he said he was alone. The man saw Jim's only weapon, a knife slung low on his waist.

Jim had been using a knife for hunting all his life. He was as accurate with a knife as with a gun. But the two men did not know that. They were laughing to themselves. Here was a plain old back woodsman with money in his pocket. It could be theirs for the taking.

The sun was sinking low in the sky. Shadows from the buildings fell across the street. All eyes were on the three men as they turned toward a boarding house. Jim knew something was wrong. Talk among the men sitting in the shade of the buildings became whispers. The laughter stopped. Occasionally an old-timer moved his tobacco from one cheek to the other and spit on the dry, crusty ground.

The three men walked slowly, talking quietly. As they passed an open space between two buildings, the two men quickly pushed Jim into the dark space. One of the men had a revolver. The other demanded Jim's money. Before either man could move, Jim ducked low, grabbed the gun with one hand and flashed his knife in the other hand.

No one could see what happened. There were groans and sounds of fighting. The two well-dressed, friendly men did not look so happy as they ran back into the street. Their clothes were slashed. Blood dripped from their hands. They looked wildly both directions before running toward the livery stable.

Jim walked calmly back to the street. He stood for a moment and watched the two running men. Very gently he wiped his bloody knife on his ragged pants leg. No one spoke as he once again headed toward the boarding house.

After two days in New Orleans Jim looked like a different man. With new clothes, a bath, a haircut, and a shave, he made a dashing figure. Men were impressed with his good business sense. Women were anxious for him to meet their unmarried daughters.

Jim knew he would like living in New Orleans, but he wasn't quite ready to make another move. He needed more money before he could have the power he wanted in New Orlean's society. Jim knew that he had impressed some people. That wasn't enough. He wanted to be an equal in every way. He could do that only if he had money and a reputation to back it.

No one cracked a smile as the comic figure came from behind the livery stable. A well-dressed, distinguished-looking young man sat astride a young, spirited, gray mule. The mule's pointed ears stood straight up. It had a wild look about its eyes. The young man sat relaxed on its bare back. His long legs dangled near the ground.

As Jim turned the mule toward home, the men along the street grew still. They saw the knife Jim had used. It was hung in a scabbard low on his waist. The end of the scabbard was tied by straps to Jim's right thigh.

Jim's face was serious but his eyes were full of laughter. He knew he was a funny sight. Anyone could laugh with him. His look dared anyone to laugh at him.

As he neared the end of the street an old-timer chuckled and asked, "What's your name, son?"

"Jim Bowie" was the stout reply.

Jim knew he would be remembered in New Orleans. He did not know how often the story of his visit would be told. The legend of Jim Bowie and his use of a knife had begun.

III

The Deadly Duelist

Jim spent five years clearing his land. He was a good farmer and businessman. He made money from his farm. He met strangers easily. He was at ease with men of high society as well as renegades. Jim was often invited to the best homes in New Orlean. He was found frequently in saloons laughing and joking with the roughest, toughest men in the city.

Each time he took lumber to New Orleans, he made new friends. Jean Lafitte, a renegade pirate who captured slave ships, often entertained Jim. Jim knew that Lafitte as well as the wealthy businessmen respected him. He had become their equal in reputation.

Jim did not spend money needlessly. When he was in the city, he dressed and acted the city dandy. When he returned to his farm, he lived with basic necessities. He needed money to be a big-time landowner.

One day Jim walked over his well-developed farm. He was no longer shut off from other people. The wilderness around his property was settled. He could hear the echo of voices and saws. The old restlessness within him began to rise again. The challenge to conquer his land had been fulfilled.

The value of Jim's farm had greatly increased. The land was cleared of trees and brush. Fields had been neatly furrowed and planted. A well built house and barn sat on a rise in the land. Tall pine trees sheltered the homestead. The time was right to sell.

Jim sold his farm at a large profit. He now had money to invest. If he could continue to buy and then sell at a gain, he could enlarge his wealth.

Jim went to see Resin. He still had dreams of their being partners. Resin was settled, but he had enough of the Bowie spirit to want a little excitement. They put their monies together and began developing sugar plantations in Louisiana.

The two brothers made good partners. Resin liked to stay close to home. Jim liked to travel and explore. Resin took care of the business while Jim searched for more land to buy. They owned several valuable estates between the years 1819-1828. The sugar plantations were bought, improved, and sold for more money than the brothers had invested. Their wealth grew.

Jim and Resin were always interested in making money. In addition to their sugar plantations, they had another interest. John, their oldest brother, joined them in business. The three Bowie brothers began to deal in slave trade.

Slave trade was illegal in the South. Jim was friends with John Lafitte, who was notorious for his slave trade business. Lafitte captured slave ships and carried the slaves to Galveston Island.

John purchased small boats and stocked them with necessary food and supplies. Jim took the boats to Galveston Island to pick up slaves. He paid Lafitte $140 for each slave. Since slave trade was illegal, Jim said he found the slaves and took them to the custom officer for a reward.

The law was very irregular. Sometimes the rules were enforced and other times they were ignored. There was always a question of what to do with the slaves once they had been smuggled into the United States. Most of the southern states sold the slaves to the highest bidder.

Resin bought the slaves that Jim turned in and resold them at a profit. Within three years they cleared $65,000 over their investment.

The profit was invested in sugar plantations. The largest and best estate was Arcadia. Resin and his family made the beautiful old home the finest in that part of the country. Jim spent much of his time there between his trips.

Jim and Resin were wealthy businessmen. They were respected. Resin was accepted in community and state politics. Jim was known throughout Louisiana and Mississippi as a fair but dangerous man. With the large profit made in the slave trade business, they had extra cash. They had made names for themselves.

Jim and Resin decided to give up the slave trade business. They had a new idea that they wanted to try at Arcadia Plantation. They could afford to gamble on new ideas.

Both Jim and Resin were good at working with their hands and repairing mechanical equipment. They could save money if they could grind their own sugar cane. On Arcadia Plantation they developed the first steam mill for grinding sugar cane ever used in Louisiana.

Resin was satisfied with improving sugar plantations. He loved to speak before audiences. His speeches were well-planned and well-delivered. He became an orator and was involved in Louisiana politics.

Jim was different. When he accomplished one thing, he didn't want to do it again. He moved on to something new. He was bored with sugar plantations. He roamed the country, unable to settle down.

Talk about his fights and scrapes floated back to Resin. Resin loved Jim as a friend and a brother. He was worried that one day Jim would not return. The stories that came back to Resin were generally about Jim's use of a hunting knife.

One day Resin walked briskly from the house to the blacksmith's shop on Arcadia Plantation. For days he wandered in and out of the hot, barnlike building. The blacksmith was secretive about what he was doing. No one but Resin was allowed near his workbench.

Several days later, Resin came from the blacksmith's shop. He had something hidden in his hands. The sparkle in his eyes was the only clue to his excitement. He walked to a grove of trees past the plantation house. With his back to the house, he looked at the object he was holding.

Resin turned the knife over slowly in his hand. It was designed for hunting, butchering, and dueling. The knife was sharp and thin on one edge, ending in a sharp slender point. The back side of the point curved into a concave arc. A guard to protect the hand separated the handle and the eight inch razor-sharp blade.

Resin looked over his shoulder to be sure he was alone. He held the knife by its slender point. Standing firm, he threw it. A soft, whirring noise ended quickly as it struck a tree. Resin walked slowly toward the tree and pulled out the knife he had designed for his brother. He shook his head in satisfaction.

When Jim returned to Arcadia, he sensed his brother's excitement. Resin was impatient to get Jim alone. After the evening meal with Resin's family, the two men walked around the plantation. Resin eventually led the way to the grove of trees.

Without a word, he took the knife from inside the coat. He pulled the long blade from the scabbard he had made. Pointing to a knot on a tree, he threw the knife. He stood where he was as Jim ran toward the tree. The knife had struck about two inches above the knot.

Jim pulled the knife from the tree. He moved it from hand to hand. He walked toward Resin. Suddenly he turned and threw the knife with a whip-like motion of the hand. Resin stared at his brother. Jim had hit dead center of the knot.

"It's yours," Resin said.

"Yah-hoo!" yelled Jim. He sounded like he did when he was a kid and rode alligators and wild broncs.

Jim gave Resin a bear-hug that could have broken Resin's ribs. Jim placed the knife in the scabbard. He unbuckled the belt that held his old knife. As he slipped the new one in its place, he knew he would never be dressed without it.

As always, after Jim rested at Arcadia a few days, he was ready to travel again. During his travels he had made friends in Mississippi as well as in Louisiana. He left to go to Natchez, Mississippi. There he fought his first duel with his newly designed knife.

The Sandbar Duel wasn't Jim's fight. The actual duel was between Doctor Thomas Maddox and Samuel Levi Welles. Maddox challenged Welles because of personal and political disagreements. The sight chosen for the duel was a sandbar near Natchez. Jim was Welles attendant for the duel.

Maddox had made the challenge. Welles had chosen the weapons. They used long barreled hand guns. The gun fired one time and had to be reloaded. Each man was allowed one shot. Jim was concerned for his friend. The argument was silly, certainly not worth killing someone. Welles would not back down. He had accepted the challenge.

Jim watched as the two men stood back to back. They paced off the distance, turned, and fired. As the smoke cleared, Jim ran to his friend. Welles was smiling. Maddox was standing but there was no smile on his face. Neither man was wounded.

Jim and Welles walked toward Maddox and Major Morris Wright, Maddox's attendant. It was the attendants' job to negotiate handshakes to show no hard feelings. The attendants would work out an agreement that was acceptable to both duelists. The duelists would then shake hands to seal the agreement. Many duelists were so glad to have escaped with their lives, they were perfectly willing to forget the entire argument.

Jim was totally unprepared for Wright's reaction to the duel. As Jim stretched his long arm to shake hands with Wright and begin negotiations, Wright drew his sword cane and struck him. Jim was stunned as he saw the blood spurt from his shoulder. He fell to his knees. Wright backed up and then lunged toward him. Before he could make another thrust with the sword, this time a deadly one, Jim threw his knife. Both men fell into blood-splattered sand. Jim was severely wounded. Wright was dead.

Jim was taken to Angus McNeil's home to

21 ARGYLE ELEMENTARY
LIBRARY

recover. McNeil was Jim's closest friend in Natchez. Jim stayed with him when he was in Mississippi. McNeil's home was always open to him.

For days Jim was severely ill with fever and infection from the wound. Dr. William Richardson attended him during the weeks of his illness. They became close friends. Dr. Richardson told Jim about the blacksmith in Natchez. He was considered the best in the trade.

Jim had a long time to think while he was recovering from his wound. He knew the story of the duel would spread across the country. He looked at the knife that Resin had designed. It was his trademark. Jim sent for the blacksmith.

When Jim rode away from McNeil's home, he was wearing his new knife. The blacksmith had copied Resin's design. The knife was forged in the finest steel the blacksmith could find. The new knife was equal to the strength of the man who wore it.

Jim Bowie, as many of the frontiersmen, believed it was right to kill anyone who needed to be killed. He did not question his ability to judge who needed killing. He always kept within the laws of the day. Many times he went before judges and jurors to be acquitted of his actions. More often than not, he was praised for his actions. He was considered to be fair in combat—and deadly.

The Bowie knife became a legend. It was reproduced in England. For some the knife symbolized illegal violence. For those who knew Jim, it symbolized right triumphing over wrong. Stories about Jim and his knife were told again and again. People knew about Jim Bowie before they ever met him. The legend of the knife preceded him wherever he went. Jim Bowie bowed down to no one.

IV

A Texas Citizen

Jim had gained the reputation he wanted. Men respected and feared him. The image of Jim's knife was stamped on men's minds. They watched closely to catch glimpses of the knife as he casually brushed his coat back. They stole glances at it when he was in buckskins with the knife hanging openly. They knew they would not see Jim without his knife.

Jim had proven his ability to use the knife. No one challenged him. At least no one who wanted to live challenged him. He became the protector of the weak against the mighty.

Jim sometimes took a ship from Natchez to New Orleans. He liked to gamble and there were always games on the ships. One evening, he walked into the gaming room and looked around. There was a poker game going between two men. Several people stood around the table. A young woman with a stricken look about her face watched the players.

The two players contrasted sharply. One was a young man, neatly dressed in a dark brown suit. His hair was parted in the middle of his head and slicked down behind his ears. Small, pale hands trembled as he wiped the perspiration from his clean-shaven face.

His eyes nervously darted from the cards being dealt to the dealer and back.

The dealer, the other player, was elegantly dressed. His pin-striped suit with a red vest gave his pudgy face a pink tint. He was slick-looking, oily, like he never took a bath but used sweet smelling water. His small beady eyes never left the young man's face while he dealt the cards. Nimble fingers slid the cards across the table.

The young man's face was grim. The gambler was smiling.

Jim went unnoticed by the people in the room. He watched the game intently. His eyes missed nothing as the gambler won again and again. Cards were dealt by the gambler. Hand after hand the young man lost. As his money dwindled, he became desperate. He increased his bidding until his last stack of money was bet on the final round. The gambler chuckled and turned over his cards.

The young woman burst into tears and ran from the room. The young man, pale and shaken, stood up to follow. A large man stepped up beside him and laid a hand on his arm.

"I think this gentleman owes you some money, son," he drawled in a slow easy voice.

"Who says?" snarled the gambler, but the smile had left his face.

A long hand brushed back the coat of the large man to reveal a knife.

"Jim Bowie's the name," he stated firmly.

The gambler raised both hands and stood up. His chair fell backwards but he made no move to grab it. His face broke into small beads of perspiration as he backed from the room.

The ship made an unscheduled stop at the next

town. Jim and the happy young couple watched as the gambler was taken to shore in a small rowboat. The story of Jim Bowie's heroism spread. Those who did not know his face knew his name.

Jim was welcomed wherever he went. He had no problems dealing with businessmen. He was good in managing money. Since he was spending more and more time in New Orleans, he established an office for his land speculations. He expanded his interest to investing other people's money in land. His friends respected and trusted his judgement.

But Jim did have a problem. He was a handsome bachelor. He was asked to dine in many of the homes with unmarried daughters. Sometimes he thought the daughters looked very much like the old bullfrogs he had turned loose in his mother's kitchen.

He did wine, dine, and court many beautiful women. None of them claimed his heart or attention for very long. Jim wasn't ready to settle with a family of his own.

The west always called him. He loved living in the wilderness. He never tired of exploring. He easily slipped from the soft life of the city dandy in New Orleans to the harsh life of the back woodsman living off the land.

One day in the late fall of 1827, Jim walked up and down the main street in New Orleans. He spoke to several people but seemed preoccupied. There was a restlessness about him. Jim was thinking about the stories he had heard of the Lost San Saba Mine in Texas.

When San Antonio de Bexar was just a mission in Texas, some Spaniards had brought silver to trade for supplies. They reported a vast silver vein ran through the mountains to the southwest. The

Spaniards had built a mission and were trying to make friends with the Indians in that part of the country.

The Apaches were warlike people. They were angry that their tribe was being pushed from their land. They attacked the Spanish forts and missions all along the San Saba River. They destroyed everything in their path. They covered all clues to the entrance of the silver mine. No one knew the mine's location.

Jim made up his mind. With the same determination that he tackled his first farm, he decided to move west again. There was excitement in his face. His eyes sparkled with visions of another wild country. A new adventure was waiting for him.

Texas was a newly opened country. American colonists had gotten permission to move into the Mexican ruled territory. San Antonio de Bexar was the center of activity.

As Jim traveled toward Bexar, later to be called San Antonio, he saw land, land, land that was unsettled. He went from thick woods to open prairie on his trip. He went for days without seeing another person.

Once Jim came upon an Indian hunting party. The Indians were mostly young braves looking for game to take to their camp for food. Jim discovered that one of the young men spoke Spanish. He explained that he was going to San Antonio de Bexar.

The Indians invited him to go hunting with them. Jim, remembering the stories of the lost mine, spent several days hunting. He hoped he would get a clue to the location of the mine. If the Indains knew, they carefully guarded their secret. Jim made friends among the Indians, but he learned nothing about the mine. The Indians learned that Jim used a knife better than any white man they had ever seen.

By the middle of June, 1828, Jim had set up his headquarters in Bexar. He was disappointed to find that he could not speculate in land until he fulfilled three requirements. He had to become a Catholic, a Texas citizen, and produce a letter of recommendation.

Becoming a Catholic was no problem for Jim Bowie. He was immediately accepted into the society of wealthy Mexican citizens. The church required a person joining to have two sponsors. Jim asked Juan Martin and Joseph Navarro de Veramendi, both respected and wealthy citizens, to sponsor him. On June 26, 1828, Jim was baptized into the Roman Catholic Church.

The letter of recommendation had to be written by someone who had known Jim for some time. There were no mail services. The only way messages were delivered was if someone happened to be going in the direction the message was to be sent. That meant Jim would have to return to Louisiana for the letter.

He was in no hurry. Texas was where he wanted to stay. He spent four months exploring Texas so he could choose the land he wanted when the time came. That was also a good excuse to roam the countryside.

The Lost San Saba Mine was always on Jim's mind. He took several hunting trips with the Indians. He never asked about the mine. He knew the Indian hunters would become suspicious of him. He was an excellent hunter. They respected and trusted him. He didn't find the mine, but he knew he would keep looking for it.

When Jim finally returned to Louisiana, he

wanted Resin to move to Texas. Resin was involved in state politics. He had his home and family there. He was settled and wanted to stay that way.

Jim sold most of his business interests there and was back in Texas in February, 1830. He carried a letter of recommendation in his pocket. Thomas F. McKinney, a boating and trade merchant from New Orleans, wrote Stephen F. Austin, who was in charge of the American colonists in Texas. McKinney assured Austin that Bowie was highly respected by all who knew him. He stated that Bowie wanted to become a Texas citizen and would promote Texas' general interests.

Austin accepted Bowie as a colonist. On February 10, James Bowie took the oath of citizenship. He promised to comply with the Federal and State Constitutions of Texas and Mexico and to observe the Catholic religion. Two days later he applied for land on Galveston Island.

Stephen F. Austin introduced Jim into the governmental society at Bexar. He was elected a colonel in the Texas Rangers. The influential families welcomed him in their homes. He was popular with all classes of people and known throughout the town.

Jim applied for many land grants, but he never lived on the land. He still had vivid memories of the stretched muscles and aching back when he cleared his first farm. He had no visible means of support, yet he lived lavishly. His dress was of the finest quality. He entertained in the best manner of the day.

Jim frequently watched the Mexican children playing in the plaza. One day a fight broke out among them. Suddenly, all of the children except two small boys withdrew. The children stepped back to form a line on each side of the boys. Jim was amused to see the two boys immitating him.

In one hand each held a tattered sombrero for a shield, in the other a homemade Bowie knife carved of wood. With legs apart and feet firmly on the ground, the boys faced each other. A set look was on their faces. The children around them were quiet.

Jim quickly stepped into the fighting line between the duelers. With his hands on his hips, he looked first at one boy and then at the other.

"¿Qué tal?" he drawled.

The children scampered like frightened rabbits and were out of sight before he could utter another word.

Jim smiled. He lazily looked around him. The bustle and rythm in the town captivated him. The town was growing. There was direction in its movements. Under all the civilization there was an excitement of some pending adventure. Jim's eyes moved slowly up the rough stone street to rest on the Alamo. Its large structure loomed against the sky to give permanence to the rapidly changing town.

Jim Bowie had found his home. Here he would live—and here he would die.

V

A Family Begins

Jim was truly a citizen of Texas. He was a colonel
in the Texas Rangers. Mexicans and Americans had
accepted him in their societies. He fit as easily with
one as with the other. Many of the Indians were his
friends.

Jim's days were filled with business transactions
and roaming the countryside, generally looking for
the Lost San Saba Mine. He still hunted with the
Indians. They sometimes took him to their
campgrounds after a successful hunt. Jim watched the
women and children greet the hunters upon their
return. He wished there was someone to welcome his
return at Bexar.

Don Juan Martin de Veramendi had opened his
home to Jim. He treated Jim like a son. It still wasn't
the same as Jim's having a home of his own.

Veramendi was the vice-governor of Coahuila-
Texas. He and Doña Josefa, his wife, lived with their
children in the governor's palace on Soledad Street.
Jim had eaten many meals at their house. The
children were always silent during Jim's visits. They
were in awe of him.

Jim and Veramendi discussed business.

Veramendi was wealthy and influential. He gave advice to Jim and often asked advice from Jim on business matters. Occasionally as the men talked, Jim caught Ursula, Veramendi's oldest daughter, stealing glances at him. When he smiled at her, she dropped her eyes and slipped from the room. She was a shy child.

One day in August, 1830, Veramendi sent for Jim to come to the governor's palace. He looked grim when Jim arrived. Ramón Musquiz, the political chief of Bexar, sat in a chair by Veramendi's long, wooden desk. Jim looked at Musquiz. Musquiz dropped his eyes to stare at the floor.

Jim was puzzled. Why would Musquiz feel awkward seeing him? The political chief was the law officer of Bexar. His job was to deal with people who had broken the law.

Veramendi handed Jim a letter. As Jim read the document, his face paled. It was a warrant for his arrest. He was accused of killing and robbing a settler.

Each of the American colonies had established its own governing body. The letter was from an alcalde (mayor) from a colony near the Louisiana border.

Jim looked at the pained face of his good friend, Veramendi.

"I am not guilty," he stated.

Veramendi sat quietly and thought. It was true that Jim Bowie had a reputation as a fighter. There was no question that he had killed men. But hadn't the men deserved killing? Had he any reason to doubt Jim's honesty? He had none!

"I will take Jim to Satillo and on to Monclova," Veramendi said as he looked at Musquiz. "If Jim is not here, you cannot arrest him."

Musquiz looked relieved. He stood and looked

up at the tall man beside him. Jim was his friend but he was also deadly in duel. He did not want to force a fight between them. He took the paper from Jim's hand and folded it. No one would know about it until Jim was away from Bexar.

Satillo, Mexico, was the headquarters for Veramendi's Mexico business ventures. He often relied on Jim's advice in its operation. After they spent several days checking on the business, they went on to Monclova where the Veramendi family had a summer home.

Jim and Veramendi spent many days discussing business. Jim wanted to invest in cotton mills. They decided to become partners. Machinery for cotton mill establishment in Satillo was ordered from Boston.

Problems confronted them. To own property in Mexico, Jim had to become a Mexican citizen. He couldn't do it with a warrant out for his arrest. James Bowie began to feel trapped.

He grew restless and wandered around the summer estate. One day as he walked back to the home, he stopped and looked at the family on the veranda. Veramendi and Doña Josefa were surrounded by their happy children. Lately Jim had become aware that Ursula was not a child.

Ursula sat listening to the chatter around her. She was not aware that she was being watched. Occasionally she would lift a long delicate hand to push a wisp of black hair back into place in the braid around her head. The fan she held moved gently back and forth to cool her beautiful face.

Jim's heart seemed to stop beating. He made a sudden movement. Ursula looked toward him. As their eyes met, Jim knew he had found his love.

Just as Jim knew he wanted to court and win Ursula, he knew that he could not ask permission to do so until his name was cleared. He began to brood.

Veramendi sensed Jim's restlessness. He suggested that he and Jim return to Saltillo to complete negotiations for the cotton mill. They were met on the way there by a lone rider. He informed them that they must report to José María Viesca, the governor of Coahuila-Texas, immediately.

They wasted no time in getting to Satillo. Viesca's face broke into a wide smile as he saw them. He handed Jim a letter. Ramón Musquiz had written from Bexar that the warrant for Jim's arrest was a mistake. The warrant should have read James Poover instead of James Bowie.

There was no mistake about the relief that passed over the faces of the men.

Governor Viesco assisted the two men in attaining Jim's Mexican citizenship. On September 30, 1830, Jim was given letters of citizenship by the congress of Coahuila-Texas. Jim could now own property in Mexico.

Jim was also free to ask Veramendi's permission to court his daughter Ursula. Although Jim was thirty-five and Ursula just nineteen, Veramendi was pleased at the match.

The family and Jim returned to Bexar. During the winter months under the chaperone of Doña Josefa, Jim won Ursula's heart. Each evening he took a bouquet of freshly cut roses to the governor's palace. As Doña Josefa sat on the patio overlooking the river, Jim and Ursula walked along the tree shaded banks.

The winter evenings were cool and clear. Ursula wrapped a heavy shawl around her shoulders. As they walked along Jim took her small, soft hand in his. A cloud passed in front of the full moon. There was a momentary darkness. Doña Josefa could not see them. Jim gently took Ursula in his arms. He softly kissed her upturned face.

Jim felt her small body tremble. He stood back and looked into her delicate face. He saw Ursula's eye lashes flutter before she shyly raised her eyes to look at him. He must persuade her to marry him.

Ursula needed no persuasion to agree to marry Jim. He was handsome and well-mannered. He treated her gently, almost as if he were in awe of her beauty. Before spring arrived, they were making wedding plans.

Veramendi and Doña Josefa happily consented to the marriage. The marriage banns were published three times on April 11th, 17th, and 24th. No objections were made to the union.

San Fernando Cathedral marked the center of Bexar life. Majestic parochial bells rang out for all occasions. The fast, high-pitched sound warned the peaceful citizens of Indians approaching. They mournfully tolled in solemn tones the death of the monarchs of Castille. On April 25, 1831, the bells rang joyously to announce the marriage of Ursula Vermendi and James Bowie.

Veramendi and Doña Josefa stood sponsors for the wedding of their daughter. Don José Angel Navarro and Don Juan Francisco Bueno were witnesses. Don Rufugio de la Garza happily performed the marriage ceremony.

Jim took Ursula to New Orleans on a wedding trip. She had never seen that part of the country. And Jim wanted to show off his beautiful bride to his friends and kindred. Ursula was considered one of the

world's rarest beauties. Jim was proud that his family and friends liked Ursula as well as admired her.

They were welcomed wherever they went. Everyone talked about what a handsome couple they made. Their good looks complimented each other. Jim was tall and fair of skin compared to Ursula's petite size and dark beauty.

After his marriage, Jim was considered by everyone in Bexar to be a son of Veramendi. He declared his wealth in his marriage contract to be $250,000. Also upon marriage to a Mexican woman, he was given a league of land which was 2,628 acres.

Jim and his father-in-law became partners in a cotton mill in Satillo. Once the operation was running smoothly, Jim lost interest. Veramendi established a residence in Satillo and divided his time between Bexar and there. That was convenient because as vice-governor of Coahuila-Texas, he had to be in Mexico frequently on political business. It suited Jim because it left him free to continue exploring and looking for the Lost San Saba Mine.

When Jim and Ursula were in Louisiana on their wedding trip, Jim had talked to Resin about coming to Texas. He explained to Resin about the lost mine. Resin was ready for a little adventure. He promised to come for a visit. By the time the Bowies got settled back at Bexar, Resin came to explore.

In the fall, the two brothers set out to find the silver mine. They took seven men and a string of pack horses. The party headed west of Bexar. Jim had not explored the mountains along the Rio Grande River. He knew it was wild and rugged country. Game was plentiful so they would have no trouble catching food.

They had been moving daily for about two weeks

when they thought they had found the mine. Traces of previous activity could be found in the underbrush. The horses were jittery. Jim decided they would camp in a valley between two mountains. There was a trail of sorts going up to the one to the south. The next day they could explore on foot and give the horses a rest.

They set up camp. Jim cleaned the wild turkey they had killed that day. Resin built a fire and banked up the coals under a spit to roast the turkey. The other men unloaded and hobbled the horses in a grassy spot to graze. The cool breeze felt good on their parched faces.

Darkness fell over the men sitting around the fire. They had eaten their fill. One by one they stretched out on their bedrolls to lie and dream. Only Jim and Resin knew they were on the brink of discovery.

The movement of the horses stamping around woke the camp with a start. Jim motioned to the men to be still. He slipped quietly out of the glow from the camp's fire. A horse whinned as Jim threw his knife with deadly aim. An Indian brave fell with the tether rope in his hand.

The men grabbed their guns and ammunition and ran for cover. Jim joined them. They secured themselves within some large boulders on the side of the mountain. Suddenly Indians were coming from three different directions.

A cloud of dust rose from under the horses hooves. The exploring party began firing. There was so much smoke and dust they could not see until an Indian was right at them. Twice Resin killed two with one shot as the Indians criss-crossed in the blaze of bullets.

The attack lasted most of the night. The Indians retreated and charged time and time again. Jim and Resin counted 160 in the war party. No one thought they could escape with their lives.

As the blackness of the night began to fade, the Indians retreated. The exploring party was exhausted. They were afraid to leave their stronghold. They saw no movement of life as the sun came up. Jim slipped quietly from his perch behind the boulder. He ran from bush to bush until he had covered the area. He waved to the men to come forward.

The horses were gone. Their supplies were trampled in the ground. Dead Indians were everywhere. Jim and Resin knew they could not press their luck. They had lost no men. They counted fifty-two dead warriors.

Quickly they salvaged what they could from their camp. They would have to try to catch stray horses on their way toward Bexar. They could stay there no longer. They didn't find the mine, but they knew where to look for it.

For two years after Resin's visit, Jim was a man of leisure. His father-in-law was taking care of his Mexico interests. Resin was running his Louisiana investments. Jim and Ursula had a beautiful baby daughter. Jim fought Indians when they went on the warpath and attacked the settlements. He took trips to try to rediscover the San Saba Mine. His days were full and happy.

Jim's happiness was short-lived. In the summer of 1833, Jim had to return to New Orleans to take care of business. He did not like leaving Ursula behind. They had a small daughter and Ursula was pregnant again.

Jim heard rumors that cholera, a serious and

often fatal disease, was spreading across Texas. He would not leave until Ursula promised to go to Monclova to the Veramendi's summer home. She was to stay until Jim returned for her. He hoped to finish his business quickly and return before the birth of their second child. Ursula, her daughter and parents left for Monclova. Jim went to Louisiana.

Jim was not present when his second child, a son, was born in August. Ursula was excited as she looked at the infant in her arms. She knew how proud Jim would be. She watched the road daily for his return.

Ursula was worried when her son started vomiting. She sat by the window through the night holding her baby. She faced the direction that Jim would come.

Her mother, Doña Josefa, gently shook her. Ursula's head was resting on the back of the rocking chair. She slowly opened her eyes. Waves of nausea swept over her.

"Yes, Mamá?" she whispered.

"Your daughter is very sick," said Doña Josefa.

Through the long day, Ursula nursed her children. both were vomiting and crying with stomach cramps. Ursula placed them on the large bed with her. She lay with her eyes fixed on the door.

"Oh, Jim," she cried. "Please come quickly!"

Cholera swept through the Veramendi household with a passion. Within three days, Ursula, her two children, her parents, and four servants died. Just as quickly as the disease had struck, it left the household in silence.

Jim was not present when his wife and children died.

During the months that Jim had been gone, he had moved from place to place. He was settling all of his business interests in that part of the country. Texas was where his heart was. He had no contact with his family since leaving Bexar. He was anxious to see them.

Around the first of November, Jim left Natchez and headed toward home. He was going straight to Monclova to spend some time with his family before taking them home to Bexar. He traveled long hours and stopped only at night to rest.

On his trips he had made friends with settlers along the way. He was nearing the Texas border when he stopped at a friend's to spend the night. There was a message waiting for him.

Jim seemed to shrink in size as he read the message. His beautiful Ursula and children were dead. He would never see the son born to them.

With a cry of anguish, Jim ran from the room. Long into the night, sounds of chopping wood echoed in the stillness. Jim sliced the wood with one blow of the axe. The day dawned on a ravaged man sitting alone on a stump of wood.

The settlers watched as Jim saddled his horse and rode back in the direction he had come. Day after day he rode, slumped in his saddle.

Jim Bowie, the brave and the bold, had lost his desire for adventure. For the first time in his life he had no wish to discover the unknown. He was defeated.

VI

Texas Revolution

Angus McNeil looked into the grief-stricken face of the man sitting on the horse. He had seen a rider come to a stop at the gate of his garden.

"Jim Bowie!" he gasped.

He hardly recognized his friend. Not two weeks had passed since he had sent a happy Jim on his way to Monclova.

McNeil called a servant to help him. They gently lifted Jim from the weary horse and carried him into the house.

Jim had returned to Mississippi. He was despondent and ill. Angus called Doctor Richardson to help him. For weeks Jim tried to bury himself in grief. He spent the days staring into nothing. He ate little food. The big man was becoming smaller by the day.

McNeil and Richardson tried to interest him in new ventures. Nothing worked. Jim decided to sell all of his businesses. His friends tried to talk him out of it. His mind was made up.

With the same determination that Jim built his empire, he sold it. In December, against the advice of his friends, he returned to Texas and Monclova to sell his land and cotton mills. He sold all of his investments at a great financial loss to him.

Inactivity was not in Jim Bowie's nature. Once he had no interests to keep him in one place, he moved constantly. For two years he roamed Texas, Mexico, Louisiana, and Mississippi. He became a land agent for a time for John T. Mason. He showed no interests in land speculation for himself. He had no roots in any state.

In the late summer 1835, Jim, Angus McNeil, and Dr. Richardson came to Texas. Dr. Richardson had $80,000 to invest in land. When they arrived, Jim realized the extent of dissatisfaction of the Texans. They wanted to be free of the Mexican rule. Battles were already ranging between the two political powers. Jim felt a new surge of the old adventurous spirit.

He had met many of the volunteer forces. Back woodsmen from as far as Virginia and Tennessee were drifting toward the Texas fight. Jim wanted to be a part of it.

For a time, Jim was treated equally well by Mexicans and Americans. He was still a colonel in the Texas Rangers. He became aware that he was being watched closely. The Mexicans no longer trusted him, but they wanted to keep him where they knew what he was doing. He had a reputation for roaming the countryside. He was able to use the reputation to slip away from Bexar. In late September Jim joined the forces assembling at Gonzales.

The first battle in the struggle for Texas liberty from Mexico was the Battle of Gonzales fought October 2, 1835. The settlers in the community had been given a cannon to protect them from Indian attacks. The Mexicans came and demanded the cannon be given to them. Alcalde Andrew Ponton refused to surrender it.

The colonists, afraid of the cannon being taken, buried it in George W. Davis' peach orchard. Ponton sent messages to other colonists that they would not give up the cannon.

The Mexicans made their stand by the river. They would not leave without the cannon. The colonists had no ammunition for it. A plea was made for material suitable for firing. The community gathered chains and scrap iron. They dug up the cannon and mounted it on ox-cart wheels. The cannon was filled with pieces of the chains and scrap iron.

The Texans boldly pulled the cannon across the river and met the Mexican troops. The first shot of the Revolution was fired by a rusty cannon filled with rusty scrap metals. The Mexican troops retreated. One Mexican soldier was killed. No Texans were lost.

The Texas troops reassembled at Gonzales. Gonzales was the headquarters for the army. A few short battles had occurred between there and the Mexican Border. It was the collection place for weapons and clothing taken from dead Mexicans. Volunteers were furnished supplies if they needed them. Most of the volunteers came with their own clothing and weapons.

Stephen F. Austin called together the volunteer army. Jim Bowie was one of his officers. They marched toward Bexar.

The Texas Volunteer Army was a sight unlike any other. The ninety men under the command of Austin, Bowie and Fannin had no regular training. Their dress was as varied as the animals they rode.

Some of the men were wearing tattered clothes that barely hung on their figures. Some were wearing pantaloons taken from the dead Mexicans. The pantaloons were gathered at the waist and ankles. Shirt sleeves were too short to cover the wrists. Some wore buckskin breeches. The new buckskin was soft and yellow. The old was hard and black from grease and dirt. Most of the men had moccassins or shoes but few had socks.

Sombreros shaded the eyes of some. Coonskin caps with the tail hanging down behind covered the bushy hair of others. A few wore military caps. A small Spanish pony trotted beside a big American horse. A half-broke mustang pranced back and forth among the sober, methodical plodding mules.

There was no standard weapon hanging on their saddles. Each man furnished his own. Bowie knives and long single-barreled, muzzle-loading flintlock rifles were the same their fathers had used to win their independence from England.

The volunteer army had some things in common. They all had the same desire. Texas must have its independence. They were all wild and ready for fight.

The task of the volunteer army was to find the position of the Mexicans and to secure a camp for the army. Jim knew the entire area surrounding Bexar. He suggested an area near the San Antonio River. It was a well-protected defensive position for the volunteers. They were located about a mile from Nuestra Señora de la Purísima Concepción de Acuña Mission.

Jim scouted around and found about 400 Mexicans camped at the mission. He advised the volunteers to be ready to fight.

On the morning of October 28, the Mexican force attacked. The volunteers took a firm stand in the river bottom. Within thirty minutes they had killed sixty Mexicans. The Mexican troops retreated. The Texans took Concepción Mission as their campground.

Jim was pleased when the provisional government adopted a resolution praising him for heroism. He once again was feeling excitement running through his veins. His adventurous spirit had been still too long. He was ready for action.

Jim knew the locations of the Mexican strongholds in Bexar. General Cós was occupying the Alamo. He had secured buildings surrounding the area with soldiers. Jim learned the soldiers were dissatisfied. There was not enough food. They had not been paid in months. General Cós had told them that he had sent for reinforcements and pay for the troops.

Jim sent out scouting parties to watch for any communications for Cós. When a pack train was spotted about five miles from Bexar, Jim gathered about one hundred men to intercept it. As soon as the Texans were close enough, Jim ordered a charge.

Cós could see the battle from Bexar. He ordered troops with artillery to charge the Texans from behind. The main body of the Texas army had followed Jim's troop. A furious battle raged. The Mexicans retreated, but Jim captured some of the pack train.

Jim's knife glittered in the sun as he swiftly slit a pack on a burrow's back. The men gathered around were smiling. They had visions of Mexican silver and gold. Nothing fell from the pack. Jim grabbed both sides of the slit to pull it open.

Hay! Nothing but hay for the horses trapped

inside Bexar with the Mexican troops. Fifty Mexicans and one Texan killed for a pack train of hay. Jim walked slowly back to his horse.

Jim was tired. The Texans were not getting enough sleep or food. They not only had to worry about winning the battles with the Mexicans, the Indians were a threat. The Indians were always hovering in the background waiting to take victory over the wounded victors.

The regular Texas soldiers were drifting back to their homes. Frontiersmen, looking for adventure and action, were drifting into the camp. Many of them, as well as Jim Bowie, were already legends on the frontier.

The capture of the Alamo from Cós was accomplished because of the very nature of the wild frontiersmen. The regular Texas army led by General Edward Burleson was ready to return to Gonzales. Many of the men were unhappy about the decision. A captured Mexican soldier reported that the spirits within Cós' camp were low.

Burleson ordered the Texans to load the artillery for the trip to Gonzales. Ben Milam, a volunteer and renegade, was angry. He argued with Burleson. The Texans should storm the Alamo. Burleson refused.

Milan looked at Burleson and then at the men. He stepped forward, faced the volunteers and shouted, ''Who will go with old Ben Milam?''

Without any planned strategy about two hundred volunteers attacked the Mexican forces. The battle was the volunteer's kind of fighting. Each worked as an individual stalking game. They ran and jumped from house to house ambushing and attacking the Mexicans. They loved the man to man combat—fighting to kill.

The Mexicans were baffled. They had never fought that way before. After six days of fighting an unseen enemy, Cós surrendered on December 11, 1835.

When the Texans settled into the Alamo, Jim went to Goliad. He was worried. The Texans occupied Goliad and Bexar. They were convinced the war was over. Many soldiers were going home. The defenses were down. Jim had lived among the Mexicans and been considered a son. He knew they were not giving up.

Sam Houston was Jim's friend as well as commander. Jim hoped to convince him to reorganize their forces. Houston had faith in Jim, but he felt the troops should draw back from Bexar. He asked Jim to return to Bexar with a message for James Clinton Neill.

Neill was regular army. Sam Houston had put him in charge of the Bexar district. Jim carried orders for Neill to destroy the fortifications at Bexar and return to Gonzales.

When Jim arrived at the Alamo, he found Neill had only 104 men left. There were weapons but a short supply of powder. Food was scarce. There were no teams to move the artillery. But Jim had never intended to give up the Alamo.

On February 2, 1836, Jim wrote Governor Smith: "The salvation of Texas depends in great measure on keeping Bexar out of the hands of the enemy. Colonel Neill and myself have come to the solemn resolution that we would rather die in these ditches than give them up."

Governor Smith sent Lieutenent Colonel Travis with about thirty men to the Alamo. Neill received word that his wife was gravely ill. He had to return home. The command of the troops was passed to Travis.

Jim was angry. The volunteers were angry. They obeyed no one but Jim. He was in command of his troops. Jim had a better reputation for fighting than Travis. The volunteers wanted a leader that was as daring as they were.

Travis knew that Jim was angry. He understood why. Jim was older and more experienced than he was. Jim had made the decision to hold the Alamo.

Travis felt the tension among the men. He watched until he could speak to Jim alone.

One evening Travis slipped into the barracks where Jim lay on a cot. He knew that Jim was worried and had not been feeling well. In a quiet voice, unheard by the men, Travis asked Jim to continue commanding the volunteers.

Travis was trained to go by the rules of the army. Jim had always been with the volunteers. He knew their way of fighting. Jim also knew the way of the Mexicans. Travis suggested they share in the command of the men as they took refuge in the Alamo.

Jim listened to the sincere way Travis was speaking. He realized that Travis had not understood the situation at the Alamo when he was ordered to come. He sat up on the cot and held out his hand.

"I'll work with you," Jim said. "It will be better if the men see us together."

Eyes turned to watch the two men when they walked from the barracks. The men nodded to each other as Jim and Travis shook hands before parting.

Jim scouted the area around Bexar daily. He organized his men in groups to guard the mission and to watch for Mexican troops approaching. Travis tried to get him to rest more. Jim coughed constantly. He would not give up. The Mexicans were on their way.

As the Mexican troops drew nearer, the group inside the Alamo grew in determination to make a stand. The men took turns standing guard. Those who weren't guarding the fort made preparations to battle. Powder and weapons were stacked at points of strongholds. The women who had taken refuge at the mission cooked meals and prepared bandages. Everyone worked silently and quickly. The Mexicans must not know how few there were against them.

Jim and Travis had become good friends. Travis wrote Governor Smith for additional troops. He had ended his message with "Victory or Death!" They were of kindred spirits.

After days of trying to keep it from the men, Jim had to admit he was ill. Breathing was difficult for him. His muscles ached. His chest felt like a tight band had been placed around it. His body, shivering in the cold drizzle, felt hot to the touch.

The Mexican troops had arrived. Santa Anna was a professional soldier. Rain would not stop him. He pressed on with a vengence. Cós had disgraced him by giving up Bexar. Santa Anna demanded surrender of the Alamo.

Jim and Travis answered with a cannon shot. Jim knew Santa Anna would not retreat. He looked at his men with glazed eyes. He no longer had the strength to command them. His thoughts were jumbled. Full command of the Alamo defenders was passed to Travis.

Santa Anna surrounded the Alamo. For thirteen days 187 men held back 5,000 Mexicans.

Jim lay on a cot in the shelter of the chapel. The

noise of the raging battle sometimes registered in his fevered head. He opened his eyes as his hands felt cold metal. Travis had slipped a pistol under Jim's left hand. Davy Crockett had wrapped the fingers of his right hand around his knife.

The two men gently picked up Jim's cot and carried him to the dark corner of an inside room. No words were spoken as they raised their hands in salute. Jim heard the whimpers of the women and children who huddled together in fear.

The sounds of fighting became deafening. The quiet that followed was ghostly. Jim looked with blurred vision as the door to the room flew open. Two Mexicans rushed toward him. The gleaming smiles faded as Jim fired the gun. A man fell at the foot of the cot. The other fired into the man on the cot. A knife flashed from Jim's hand to end in a thud as it hit the man's chest.

Jim's search for adventure had ended.

Women and children cried as the bodies of the dead defenders were piled on a bed of tree branches. They were shocked silent when the fire leaped toward the sky. Cinders from the fire were caught and scattered by the wind.

Jim Bowie was not dead. His spirit lived on.